Inside Magic

CLOSE-UP MAGIC

Nicholas Einhorn

rosen publishing's
rosen
central

New York

This edition published in 2011 by:

The Rosen Publishing Group, Inc.
29 East 21st Street
New York, NY 10010

Library of Congress Cataloging-in-Publication Data

Einhorn, Nicholas.
Close-up magic / Nicholas Einhorn.
    p. cm. -- (Inside magic)
Includes bibliographical references and index.
ISBN 978-1-4358-9453-2 (library binding)
1. Magic tricks—Juvenile literature. I. Title.
GV1548.E33 2011
793.8–dc22
                              2010010091

Manufactured in the United States of America

CPSIA Compliance Information: Batch #S10YA: For further information, contact Rosen Publishing, New York, New York, at 1-800-237-9932.

Copyright in design, text and images © 2007, 2009 Anness Publishing Limited, U.K. Previously published as part of a larger volume: *Magical Illusions, Conjuring Tricks, Amazing Puzzles & Stunning Stunts.*

Photography by Paul Bricknell © Anness

Contents

INTRODUCTION

Performed directly in front of the spectator, close-up magic uses small, familiar props such as coins, bills, handkerchiefs, pens, fruit, keys, string, and much more. Close-up magic is by far the most popular type of magic among amateur magicians. This is because it is accessible to everyone. It requires only the simplest of props: with a collection of inexpensive everyday objects, it is possible to perform a host of magic tricks that are very often just as impressive as those you would pay large amounts for at a magic store.

In this book, you will find over forty magic tricks. Most of these routines use ordinary objects that can be found around the house, and several of them can be performed without any preparation at all. While some use simple sleight of hand, others require a minimum amount of skill. All the tricks in this book have one thing in common: they are incredibly simple to learn. However, just because a trick is easy to learn does not mean it is easy for your friends to figure out how it is done. Don't underestimate the impression these tricks will make on your friends.

These tricks may be easy to learn, but that does not necessarily mean that they are easy to perform. There is a big difference between learning a trick in the privacy of your room and performing it convincingly in front of your friends, family, or even an audience of strangers. The only way to become really good at performing is to do it as often as possible. If you take every opportunity that comes your way, you will soon develop a skill for building a rapport with your audience and creating a memorable moment of magic for both them and you, rather than just demonstrating a few clever tricks.

Some of the greatest magicians in the world have performed many of the wonderful magic tricks in this book. Now it is your turn to learn them and begin your journey as a close-up magician.

Pen-Go

A pen is wrapped up in a piece of paper. Then the paper is slowly torn into pieces, the pen having vanished into thin air! Actually it doesn't disappear into thin air – it flies up your sleeve, but no one sees it go. The pen is on a special gimmick known to magicians as a "pull." It's best to use this trick as part of a longer sequence or routine that requires the spectator to write something.

Secret View

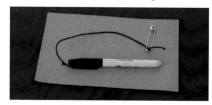

1. Attach the lid of a pen to a piece of elastic approximately 12 in (30 cm) long (depending on the length of your arm). At the other end, tie a safety pin. You will also need a piece of paper a little longer than the pen.

2. Fasten the pin inside the top of your right sleeve, so that when the elastic is loose the pen hangs just below your elbow. When you are ready to begin, you will need to pull the pen down your sleeve secretly and hold it by the cap. Pull the pen out of the cap when handing it out for use. When it is returned, re-cap the pen, making sure the elastic stays hidden behind your right wrist.

3. Begin to wrap the paper around the pen, making sure that the elastic is still hidden from view from the front. This picture shows the starting position as seen from behind, with the pen at one corner of the paper.

4. From the spectators' point of view the elastic is completely hidden by the back of your hand.

5. Wrap up the pen by rolling the paper loosely around it.

6. Hold the pen and paper loosely in your right hand.

Secret View

7. Allow the pen to slip out of the paper and up your sleeve. The tube of paper will hold its shape.

8. Rip the paper tube in half and then tear it into smaller pieces. Finally, throw the pieces of paper up in the air for a dramatic finish.

Let There Be Light

You show the spectators an ordinary lightbulb, which you then screw into your empty fist, where it immediately begins to glow. After a few seconds it "switches" off, and you hand the lightbulb to the spectators so they can check that it has not been prepared in any way. You show your empty hands and take your well-deserved applause. This trick also requires a "pull."

Secret View

1. Prepare a pull by tying one end of a piece of elastic approximately 12 in (30 cm) long (depending on the length of your arm) to a safety pin and the other end to a miniature flashlight. The flashlight needs to be one that operates at the push of a button rather than with a switch that needs to be pushed up or down. You will also require a frosted lightbulb.

2. Fasten the pin inside the top of your right sleeve so that when the elastic is loose the flashlight hangs just below your elbow. Hand the lightbulb out for examination. Meanwhile, secretly position the flashlight in your right hand, as shown above. It is important that you practice doing this in such a way that no one sees what you are doing.

3. Retrieve the lightbulb from the audience and hold it in your right hand, as shown. Show everyone that your left hand is empty, and then hold it in a fist under the bulb.

Secret View

Secret View

4. This secret view shows how the tip of the flashlight is resting against the side of the lightbulb. From the front, the audience will not be able to tell what is really happening.

5. Slowly pretend to screw the bulb into your left hand. As you do so, activate the flashlight by secretly pushing the button with the fingers of your right hand. The bulb will glow just as if it were screwed into a light socket.

6. Unscrew the light-bulb from your fist while turning off the flashlight, and show that your left hand is still empty.

7. As you are showing your left hand, release the flashlight from your right hand, allowing it to shoot up your sleeve and out of sight.

8. Finally, open both hands wide, showing the audience that there are no secret gadgets to be seen in your hands.

TIP

This could also make a great stage trick. If you wear the special pull at all times, you can even remove a bulb from a table lamp to do the trick at a moment's notice. Of course, if you do this, you must make sure the lamp is switched off and unplugged before you remove the bulb, and always replace it afterward. Also remember that if the light has been on for a while, the bulb will be extremely hot!

Coin Through Coaster

A glass is covered with a drink coaster, and a coin is visibly caused to pass through the coaster and into the glass. Performed properly, the illusion of the coin melting through the coaster is perfect. This is perhaps one of the most challenging tricks in this book, but the effect is worth the effort. You will need a glass, a coaster, two identical coins and several hours to practice and make the moves flow smoothly.

Secret View

1. Secretly hold a coin on the fingertips of your right hand, and pick up the coaster with your left hand.

2. Cover the coin with the coaster so that you are holding both the coin and the coaster in your right hand.

3. Now you need to learn a move that enables you to show both sides of the coaster without revealing the coin. As you turn your hand over to show the reverse side of the coaster, bend the fingers in, sliding the coin back so that as much of the coaster as possible is visible. Then turn your hand back, reversing the sliding motion.

Secret View

4. Display the second coin in the fingertips of your left hand, and simultaneously move the coaster toward the top of the glass. The coin under the coaster is shown here, but it must remain hidden when you perform the trick.

5. Tap the visible coin against the side of the glass as you lay the coaster on top, secretly trapping the hidden coin between the rim of the glass and the coaster. The noise from the tapping will cover any noise the hidden coin makes as it touches the rim.

6. Show the visible coin held between the finger and thumb of your right hand, while your left hand holds the coaster in place on the glass.

7. With the coin between the finger and thumb of your right hand, tap it against the coaster three times. After the third tap, squeeze the coin, flipping it sideways and pinching it so that it is hidden behind the right fingers. (This is called a "pinch vanish.") At the same moment, lift the coaster in the back with your left thumb to disengage the coin, which is then seen and heard to clink into the glass.

Secret View

8. This picture shows how things look from your side at the moment when the coin apparently penetrates the coaster.

9. As soon as you hear the coin clink into the glass, lift the coaster off the glass with your left hand.

10. Transfer the coaster to your right hand, placing it over the hidden coin, and tip the visible coin out of the glass on to the table.

11. Finally, place the coaster on the table (leaving the hidden coin underneath), and display both hands to show that they are empty.

Ring on a String

A ring penetrates a piece of string, the ends of which are both in view throughout the trick. This trick requires a ring, a safety pin and a handkerchief. It has its roots in an effect called "sefalaljia," which was created by Stewart James.

1. Show a length of string approximately 18 in (45 cm) long and lay it on the table. Borrow a ring or use your own. Lay it next to the center of the string. Then explain that by using a safety pin, you can make it look as if the ring is actually threaded on the string.

2. Cover the middle of the string with a handkerchief. Make sure both ends are clearly in view.

Secret View

3. Under the handkerchief, push a small loop of the string through the ring.

Secret View

4. Take the safety pin, and pin the left side of the loop to the string on the left side of the ring, as shown. This will leave you with the loop marked with an "x" above.

5. Put the index finger of your right hand into the loop, and hold the left end of the string with your left hand.

6. This is what it looks like from the front. Explain that the ring can't really be on the string, as the ends have not been out of sight.

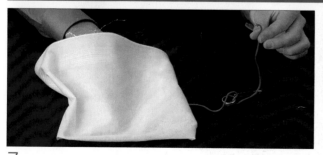

7. Pull the string to the left while keeping your right finger pressed to the table. The string will be pulled through the ring. This is covered by the handkerchief.

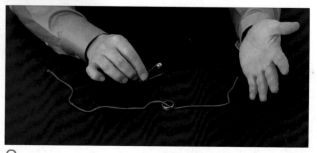

8. Finally, remove the handkerchief, undo the pin, and show that the ring really is on the string.

Chinese Coin Off String

A Chinese coin with a hole in it is threaded onto a length of string. A spectator holds both ends of the string, and yet you are able to remove the coin. This is a perfect follow-up to Ring on a String. You will see that the two tricks can easily be incorporated into a routine.

1. You need a piece of string, a handkerchief and two identical Chinese coins with holes in the middle (or you can use two matching rings instead). Hide one of the coins in your right hand: your audience must be aware of only one coin throughout the trick.

2. Thread the visible coin onto the string, and have a spectator hold both ends.

Secret View

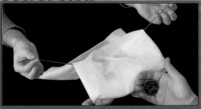

3. Cover the coin on the string with a handkerchief. This view shows the hidden duplicate coin concealed in your right hand.

Secret View

4. Under cover of the handkerchief (which has been removed here for clarity), pull the center of the cord through the hole in the middle of the loose coin.

5. Now pass this loop over the coin so that the coin hangs as shown.

6. Hide the original, threaded coin in your hand and slide it to the right, pulling the handkerchief over as you do so.

7. Slide both hands to the ends of the string: your spectator will let go. Allow the coin hidden in your right hand to slip off the cord, as you say, "Don't let go of the ends!"

8. The spectator will take hold of the ends again, but the original threaded coin is now off the string and hidden under the handkerchief.

TIP

The success of this trick relies on the spectator's release of the cord in step 7 looking like an error on his part. Don't ask him to let go, simply make it happen by moving your hands. As soon as it occurs (allowing the hidden coin to slip off), make a big deal of the fact that he shouldn't let go, and get him to hold on again. If you can make this moment look natural and keep the second coin hidden, this is a very baffling trick.

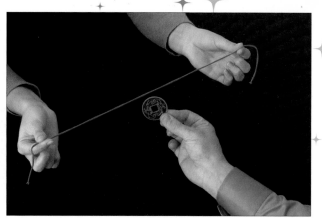

9. Put the handkerchief and the hidden coin in your pocket or to one side, keeping the coin concealed. Then slowly untie the simple knot that holds the coin on the string.

10. Finish by showing that the coin has magically passed through the string.

Rising Ring on Pencil

A borrowed ring is placed over a pencil that is held vertically by the magician. Slowly and eerily the ring begins to climb the pencil until it reaches the top. Considering how easy this trick is to do, it is incredibly effective and will fool most people.

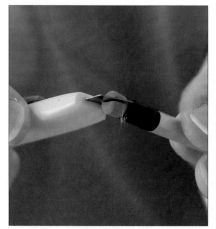

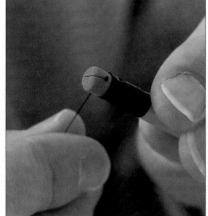

1. To set up the trick, take a pencil with an eraser on the end. With a craft knife carefully make a slit in the middle of the eraser.

2. Take a length of very thin fishing line or thread (the thinnest you can find) and tie a small knot at one end, wedging this knot into the slit. (Thick black thread was used in these pictures so that you can see how the trick works.)

3. Attach the other end of the thread to a safety pin, and fasten the pin to your belt loop or waistband. The thread should be approximately 20 in (50 cm) long, but you will need to experiment to find a length that suits you.

4. Put the pencil into your shirt pocket. Carrying it in this fashion means the thread will not get in the way.

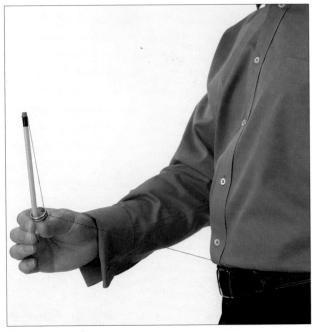

5. Remove the pencil from your pocket, borrow a ring, and drop the ring over the top of the pencil and the thread. The fine thread will remain unseen.

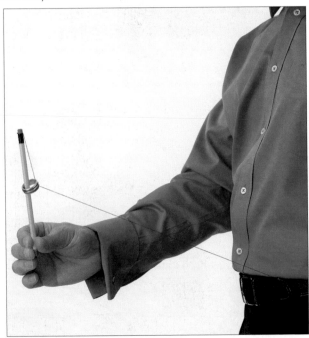

6. Put the handkerchief and the hidden coin in your pocket or to one side, keeping the coin concealed, then slowly untie the simple knot that holds the coin on the string.

7. When the ring reaches the top, remove it and hand it back to the owner. Either replace the pencil in your pocket or move the pencil away from you, secretly pulling the thread out of the eraser in order to use the pencil for something else.

Gravity-Defying Ring

A rubber band is broken and a borrowed ring is threaded onto it. The band is held between both hands at an angle of approximately 45 degrees. The ring slides up to the top of the band, uncannily defying the laws of gravity. You must try this out, as it is one of the most convincing illusions you are ever likely to see; the first time I saw it, I was completely fooled.

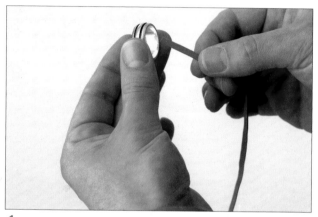

1. Choose a medium-sized rubber band with no imperfections, and break it. Hold the ring in the fingertips of your left hand and insert the top 2 cm (¾ in) of the band through the ring.

Secret View

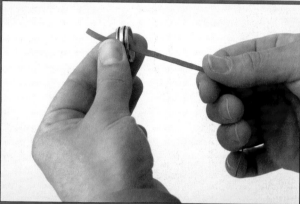

2. Notice how the rubber band is pinched between the left forefinger and thumb, with the back of the hand toward the spectators, while the ring is also pinched.

Secret View

3. Now pinch the rubber band just under the ring with your right finger and thumb.

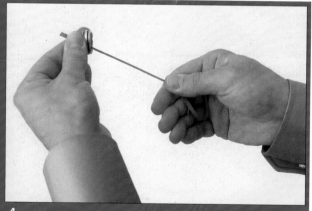

4. Pull the rubber band taut. Most of the band is hidden in your right hand.

Secret View

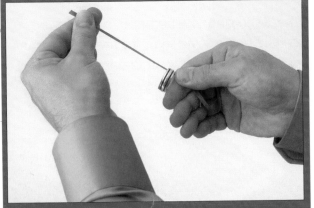

5. Allow the ring to drop down the band to rest on the index finger of your right hand.

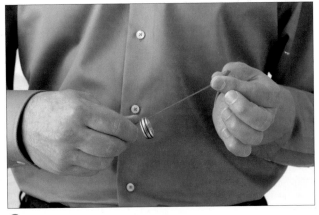

6. From the front, it looks as if you are holding the band by the two ends. In fact, what the spectators are seeing is about ¾ in (2 cm) of the band stretched to look like the entire band.

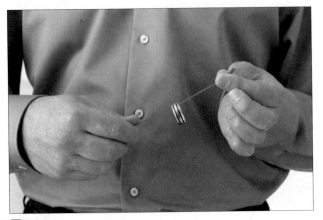

7. Hold the band at an angle of 45 degrees and slowly release the pressure of the right finger and thumb. The ring will adhere to the band. As the band retracts, the illusion is that the ring is climbing up the band.

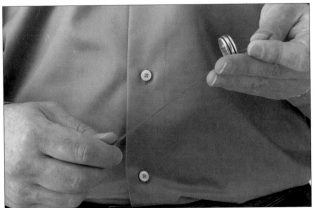

8. As soon as the band has been allowed to retract as much as possible, the fingers of the left hand complete the illusion by reaching for the ring, sliding it off the band, and handing it back to the owner.

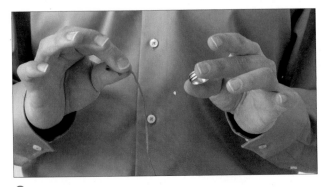

9. Finish by displaying the ring and the band, holding them in your finger. Hand them out for examination.

TIP

The band must be released slowly and smoothly for the ring to climb steadily. Experiment with different thicknesses and sizes of rubber bands, as some work better than others for this trick. The weight of the ring can also make a difference, so try using different ones. Then use the combination of ring and rubber band that works best.

Dissolving Coin (version 1)

A borrowed, marked coin is covered with a handkerchief and dropped inside a glass of water. The spectators can hear the coin plop as it enters the water, yet when the handkerchief is removed, the coin is gone. The marked coin can then be discovered in a variety of ways. For this trick you will need a small glass disc: the glass of an old wristwatch would work perfectly. You will also need a glass of water and a handkerchief. Ask someone in the audience to mark a coin with a pen so that they will be able to recognize it later.

Secret View

1. Hold a handkerchief by one corner with your left hand, with the glass disc secretly hidden under the fingertips behind the handkerchief.

2. Place the coin under the handkerchief. As your right hand comes close to the left one, allow the coin to fall into your fingers as shown, while simultaneously positioning the glass disc in the coin's place.

3. Hold the glass disc up under the handkerchief so that its outline can be seen through the material. Everyone will think this is the coin.

4. Hold the handkerchief with your left hand and position it over the glass of water. The coin is still held secretly in the right hand. Let the disc drop into the water with a plop.

5. Pull the handkerchief away using your right hand, making sure that the coin is adequately covered by the handkerchief.

6. The coin has vanished. You can even let the spectators look straight down into the glass and they will see nothing.

TIP

To reproduce the marked coin from the beginning of the trick (which will be hidden in your right hand) you can reach into a spectator's pocket and reveal the coin, creating the illusion that it somehow traveled across time and space invisibly. Or, you may want to use it to perform Marked Coin in Ball of Yarn.

Dissolving Coin (version 2)

Here is a different method for what is essentially the same trick. A coin (marked if desired) is dropped into a glass of acid, which instantly dissolves it. Do not perform both versions of this trick in the same act. Try out both, and then perform the one you prefer.

1. You will need a tall glass, a coin, a handkerchief and a bottle of water with a label that suggests that the contents are dangerous.

2. Pour some of the liquid from the bottle into the glass, explaining that it is a very strong acid that will dissolve anything it touches (except for glass, of course).

3. Show the coin to the audience, and hold it in the center of the handkerchief with your right hand. Pick up the glass with your left hand. Notice how the glass is held.

4. Move the handkerchief over the glass, and position the coin above it.

Secret View

5. This secret view shows how the glass is tipped forward and how the coin is actually positioned behind it. Let the coin fall in the direction of the arrow.

6. As the coin falls it will hit the side of the glass before resting in your left hand. The spectators will hear the coin hit the glass and assume it went inside.

7. As this shot from the front shows, the spectators cannot see that the coin is now in your left hand.

Secret View

8. As you pick up the edge of the handkerchief to remove it from the glass, secretly pick up the coin from the palm of your left hand using the fingertips of your right hand.

9. With the coin now hidden under the handkerchief, you can remove the handkerchief from the glass completely to show that the coin has vanished. Explain that the acid has dissolved it.

Coin Through Ring

A coin is placed under a thick handkerchief. The corners of the handkerchief are gathered together and threaded through a finger ring smaller than the coin, securing the coin inside. The magician causes the coin to pass through the handkerchief, freeing the ring.

1. Hold a handkerchief by one corner in your left hand and a coin in the fingertips of your right hand.

2. Cover your right hand and the coin with the handkerchief, and remove your left hand.

Secret View

3. Secretly gather a pinch of material behind the coin. This pinch is held with the thumb of your right hand.

4. Raise the front of the handkerchief with your left hand to show the coin underneath. At the same time secretly grip the back of the handkerchief between the thumb and forefinger of your left hand.

5. Cover the coin again with the handkerchief, but secretly carry both layers of the handkerchief forward.

6. This close-up view shows that the coin is now really on the outside of the handkerchief.

7. Twist the handkerchief several times under the coin. The fabric will twist around, hiding the ring.

8. Ask someone to hold on to the coin through the handkerchief. If you keep the "open" side down, no one will suspect the coin is actually on the outside. Gather the four corners of the handkerchief, and thread them through a finger ring, pushing it up to the coin.

9. Take back the covered coin from the first person. Ask two people to hold two corners each and to stretch out the handkerchief, as shown.

10. Reach underneath the handkerchief, and remove the coin from within the folds.

Secret View

11. This picture shows from underneath how the coin is removed from the folds of the handkerchief.

12. Release the coin and the ring so that the two people are left holding only the empty handkerchief.

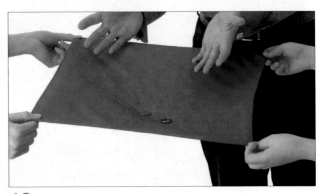

13. Finish the trick by tossing both the ring and the coin onto the stretched-out handkerchief.

Vanishing Coin in Handkerchief

A coin is clearly seen wrapped in the center of a handkerchief. With a magical gesture the handkerchief is pulled open to reveal that the coin has completely vanished. This simple and impromptu trick is one of the very best you could ever learn. Try it now and you will amaze yourself, as the coin seems to disappear into thin air! It is one of the few tricks where the secret is almost as amazing as the trick itself.

1. Lay a handkerchief in front of you in the shape of a diamond. Place a coin just a tiny bit to the left of the center.

2. Fold the bottom half up to meet the top, and pick up the right hand corner of the triangle that is formed.

3. Now fold the right side over to meet the left. The coin should not move during either of these folds.

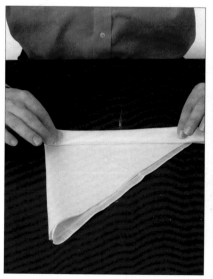

4. Pinch the coin inside the handkerchief with your right hand and slowly turn the coin over and over, rolling up the handkerchief as you do so.

5. Continue rolling up the handkerchief until you reach the top.

6. Grip the two pointed ends, one in each hand, and slowly pull them apart.

7. The coin has vanished! Actually, it is inside a secret fold, but no one would ever guess.

8. Tilt the left side of the handkerchief up so that the coin secretly runs down into your right fingers.

Secret View

9. This is an exposed view of the coin once it has landed. Notice how it sits on the fingertips.

10. Bunch the handkerchief into your right hand, covering the coin. You can finish by placing the handkerchief and coin in your pocket.

The Bermuda Triangle

Three pencils are laid on the table in the shape of a triangle. A small ship placed in the middle and covered with a glass mysteriously disappears, as does the glass. The whole trick is presented as a demonstration of how things seem to disappear inside the famous Bermuda Triangle. This trick is actually two tricks put together. You can do just the first part if you like, but running the two together makes a really great routine. The story about the Bermuda Triangle turns a basic trick into an engaging presentation.

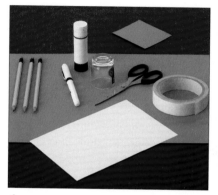

1. To set up the trick you will need several sheets of card stock, three pencils, glue, double-sided adhesive tape, scissors, a pen, a glass and a sheet of paper.

2. Trace the top of the glass on the card, and cut out a disc that exactly matches the size of the rim.

3. Glue this to the rim of the glass, making sure that no edges stick out. This special addition to the glass is known as a "gimmick."

4. Place a small piece of double-sided tape in the middle of the card disc, and press down firmly.

5. Draw a small ship on another piece of card stock, and carefully cut it out using a pair of scissors. The ship must be smaller than the surface area of the base of the glass you are using.

6. To set up the trick, arrange three pencils in a triangle on a piece of card stock that is exactly the same color as your gimmick. Place the ship in the middle. Place the glass, mouth down, on the card stock. (Notice how the gimmick becomes invisible.) Tell your spectators the legend that anything passing through the Bermuda Triangle disappears.

7. Take a sheet of plain paper. Being sure to keep the glass absolutely flat on the table, cover it as shown. The paper should not be wrapped too tightly around the glass.

8. Grip the glass through the paper and place both on top of the ship in the middle of the triangle.

9. Lift up the paper, leaving the glass on the table. The ship will have totally disappeared from view, perfectly hidden by the gimmick on the bottom of the glass. Explain that the glass represents a tornado passing through the Bermuda Triangle, and that when the tornado was directly over the ship it disappeared.

10. Re-cover the glass with the paper, then lift up the glass, gripping it through the paper. The ship will stick to the double-sided tape on the gimmick and will be lifted up with the glass.

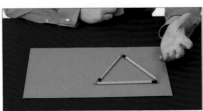

11. Explain that when the tornado moved away the ship was never seen again. Notice how the glass has been moved near the back edge of the table. While you are speaking, secretly allow the glass to slip out of the paper and into your lap. These are examples of techniques called misdirection and lapping.

12. The paper will retain the shape of the glass, even though it is no longer covering the glass. Replace this empty shell in the center of the triangle, explaining that hurricanes sometimes come back.

13. Slam your hand down on the paper, flattening it and revealing that the glass has disappeared! Pick up the paper, and explain that even a tornado can disappear in the Bermuda Triangle.

14. If you have a small box of props on a chair to your side, you can secretly take the glass off your lap and put it away as you pick up the other props from the table. Be sure to hold the sheet of card stock so that it masks the glass being secretly removed from your lap.

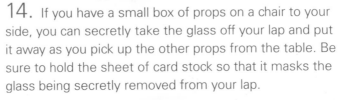

TIP
You must practice the misdirection and lapping until you can do it without thinking about it or making it obvious.

Magic Papers

A piece of folded colored paper is opened to reveal inside it another folded paper of a different color. This, too, is opened to reveal another folded paper, and this in turn is found to contain a last folded paper. When the smallest piece of paper is unfolded fully, a small coin is placed inside. The colored papers are re-folded, a magic spell is cast, and when the papers are opened once again, the contents have changed into a coin of a much larger denomination. This is handed back to the surprised and very happy donor. You will need several different colored sheets of paper for this trick. A pair of scissors or a paper cutter is also required to cut the paper to size. Using the magic papers, you can also make coins appear and vanish, as well as change their denomination.

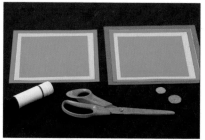

1. Using scissors, cut out a 8 in (20 cm) square of red paper. Cut out two 7 in (18 cm) squares of blue paper, two 6¼ in (16 cm) squares of yellow paper and two 5½ in (14 cm) squares of green paper.

2. Starting with a green square, fold the paper twice, to create three equal sections, as shown.

3. Fold this strip into three equal sections. Repeat these folds with each of the other papers. Make sure that the folds are neatly done and that the creases are sharp. When each paper is unfolded, it should be divided into nine equal squares.

4. Carefully glue the two blue papers back to back so that they are joined at their centers, as shown.

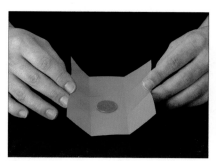

5. Place a coin of high denomination in the center of a green square. Wrap it up inside the paper, along the folds you made earlier. Place this green packet in the center of a yellow paper, and fold it inside. Finally, place the yellow paper inside the blue, and fold the blue paper around it.

6. Now assemble the other papers by laying the red paper down first, followed by the (double) blue paper, with the hidden packet containing the coin of high denomination underneath, as shown.

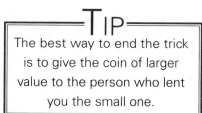

TIP

The best way to end the trick is to give the coin of larger value to the person who lent you the small one.

7. Now place the yellow paper on top of the blue and the last green paper on top of the yellow. Fold each one inside the other to complete the setup.

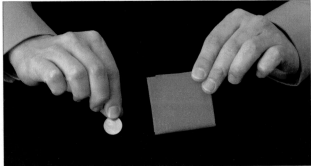

8. To perform the trick, show the packet of folded paper and a coin of low denomination. (Borrow this coin from a spectator if possible.)

9. Open the nest of papers (being careful not to reveal the underside of the prepared blue sheet) and place the low-value coin in the center of the green paper; then wrap the coin up in the green paper; then wrap this in each of the other papers in turn.

10. Secretly turn the blue paper over as you make the final fold in it.

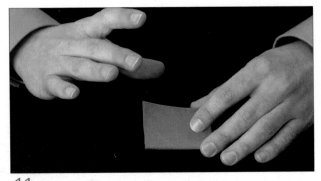

11. Wrap the blue paper up in the red paper, and cast a "mystic shadow" over the packet.

12. When you re-open the nest of papers, the coin of high denomination will be revealed.

Marked Coin in Ball of Yarn

A borrowed, marked coin vanishes, only to be discovered inside a small cloth bag in the center of a ball of yarn! This is a great trick – because it takes so long to reach the center of the ball of yarn, and the pouch is so well sealed, it seems impossible that a borrowed coin could be inside. The preparation takes some time, so start getting it ready well in advance.

1. Take a piece of thick card stock about 4 in (10 cm) wide and 4¾ in (12 cm) long. Place a large coin in the middle of the card and mark its width on the card with a pencil. Draw straight lines this distance apart along the length of the card. Draw two more lines ⅛ in (3 mm) outside the existing lines.

2. Score along the marked lines and fold to create a long, flat tube. Use glue to stick the two sides together. Press together firmly between your thumb and fingers, and allow it to dry completely before you release it.

3. When it is finished, the tube should be just big enough to allow a coin to slide along it with ease.

4. Insert one end of the coin slide into a small pouch, and hold it in place with a tightly twisted rubber band around the neck of the pouch.

5. Wrap a ball of yarn around the pouch and some of the cardboard tube.

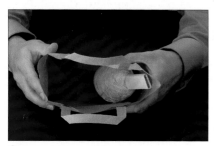

6. Place the finished article inside a paper bag, making sure that the coin slide faces upward but that it cannot be seen.

7. To perform the trick, borrow a coin, have it marked with a pen, and make it vanish using any of the methods explained in this book. Vanishing Coin in Handkerchief is ideal. Reach into the paper bag with the coin hidden in your right hand.

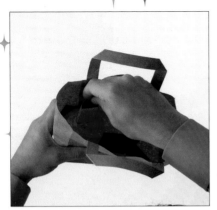

8. Secretly drop the coin into the prepared slide so that it is inserted in the bag in the center of the ball of yarn.

9. Pull the coin slide out of the ball of yarn, and leave it at the bottom of the bag as you take out the ball of yarn. You may find you need to grip the yarn through the bag with your left hand to assist in pulling out the slide.

10. Display the ball of yarn to the spectators. Squeeze it slightly as you do so, to close up the gap left by the coin slide.

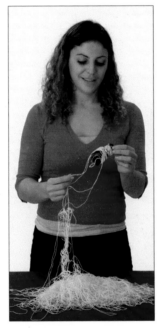

11. Ask a volunteer from the audience to unwrap the ball of yarn.

12. When she eventually finishes unraveling the yarn, which will take some time, she will discover the little pouch.

13. Ask her to verify that it is securely closed with the rubber band.

14. Ask her to open the pouch and remove the coin, and to verify that it is indeed the same coin that she marked earlier.

Coin Cascade

Ten coins are counted out loud and held by a spectator. Three invisible coins are tossed toward the spectator. When he opens his hand and counts the coins again, he now has thirteen coins! This is a great impromptu trick that can be performed almost anywhere. You can also substitute the coins for other small objects such as peanuts or candies.

1. You will need a hardback book and thirteen coins.

2. Insert three coins into the spine of the book. You will notice that when the book is closed, the coins remain hidden and are held securely within the spine.

3. Display the remaining ten coins in the palm of your hand and hold the book in the other hand.

4. Give the coins in your hand to a volunteer. Open the book somewhere in the middle, and ask the volunteer to count out loud as he places each of the coins on the book.

5. When he reaches the last coin and says "ten," tip the coins into his cupped hands. The hidden coins will slip out with the other ten coins, completely unnoticed by your volunteer.

6. Mime throwing three invisible coins toward the volunteer, and ask him how many he would have if the coins were real. He will answer "thirteen."

7. Ask the person to count out the coins onto the book once again, and to his astonishment he will indeed have thirteen coins!

TIP

A nice idea is to find a book on the subject of making money. Then when you do the trick, you can mention that the information in the book works really fast!

Concorde Coin (version 1)

In this simple yet incredibly effective trick, a coin is shown to have traveled invisibly from the right hand to the left. This is another of those rare tricks in which the method is almost as impossible as the effect. The coin really does travel invisibly from one hand to the other. For best results, perform the trick on a soft surface, such as a carpet or a tablecloth.

1. Hold a small coin in the palm of your right hand. Notice how it is positioned, just below the base of the first and second fingers. Hold your left hand palm up as well, about 10 in (25 cm) from the right hand. The backs of your hands should be close to the floor or table.

2. Now turn both hands palms down very quickly. The right hand should move a fraction of a second before the left. With practice the coin will be flicked from the right hand to the left as they turn over. The coin moves so fast that the eye cannot see it. Fortunately, the camera can.

3. Take a few moments to explain that you are going to make the coin travel from your right hand to your left hand using magic. (Of course it is all done now, but as far as the spectators are concerned, nothing has happened yet.)

4. Slowly raise your hands to show that the coin has indeed traveled across to the left hand. This really is a case of the hand being quicker than the eye.

Concorde Coin (version 2)

Here is an impressive variation of the trick above. Instead of using the surface of a table or the floor, this version can be performed standing up. The moves are identical, apart from the fact that as the hands turn over they close into fists.

1. Hold the coin in the palm of your right hand as before, and hold your left palm 10 in (25 cm) from your right hand.

2. Quickly flip your hands over, throwing the coin across to the left hand as you do so.

3. Having caught the coin, ball your hands into fists.

4. Open your hands to show the coin has traveled across.

TIP

You can add a little misdirection to improve the trick further. Start by showing the coin in your right hand, and then turn both hands over without throwing the coin. Say: "I am going to make the coin travel from my right hand to my left hand. In fact, it has already happened. But the hard thing is to make the coin travel back again … look, it's back." Open your hands and show the coin in your right hand, where it has been all along. Of course this is a silly joke, but as soon as the spectators laugh, you turn your hands over again (this time doing the secret move) and say: "No seriously, I can do it – watch." Performing it like this means that no one will see the move when you actually throw the coin because they think the trick is over. You do the move when they are least expecting it to happen.

The Coin Test

While your back is turned, someone is asked to pick up a coin from the table and hold it high in the air in either hand. When she has lowered the hand, you turn around and are able to say with 100 percent accuracy which hand holds the coin. This clever mind-reading trick is a great impromptu stunt to remember the next time someone asks you to do something "off the cuff."

1. Give someone a coin and ask her to place it in either hand while your back is turned. Then ask her to hold the coin high in the air and say "read my mind" five times.

2. When you compare her hands, one will be paler than the other. This is the one that holds the coin, since the blood will have left the hand while it was up in the air.

3. Finish by triumphantly pointing to the hand that holds the coin.

TIP

To conceal your method, you can start by asking the person to raise her right foot and then look right and left before asking them to hold up the hand with the coin. People will think every move must have some meaning and therefore won't necessarily guess the true method.

Universal Vanish

This simple sleight-of-hand trick is handy to know as you can make practically anything disappear with a wave of your hand. As with all tricks, practice is essential to make it really work well. This works best if your spectators are seated opposite you.

1. You need to be seated at a table. Have the object that is to vanish in front of you. In this case, it is a coin.

2. Turn your hand palm down so that it covers the coin and is almost flat on the table.

Secret View

3. Move your hand forward until the coin touches the heel of your hand. Make small circular motions so the coin continues to slide beneath the heel of your hand.

Secret View

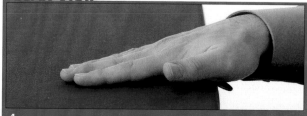

4. As the heel of your hand moves over the edge of the table, the coin drops secretly into your lap.

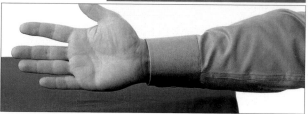

5. The hand continues to "rub" the coin, moving forward and away from the table's edge. Finally, flip your hand over to show the coin has vanished.

Gravity Vanish

This technique is another great way to make many types of small objects seemingly disappear into thin air. Its success depends largely on timing and the use of angles. It must be seen just from the front, so do not attempt to perform this trick if there is any possibility that the audience will have a view from the side, or you will give away the secret of how it is done.

1. Hold a small object (in this case a coin) in your left hand. Notice how the object is held and displayed.

2. Rotate your hand at the wrist so that the back of your hand blocks the spectators' view of the coin.

3. Count to three, each time raising a finger. Notice how the right hand comes right in front of the left hand so that it is concealed from view.

Secret View

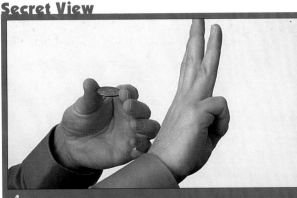

4. This view shows how things look from the side. The coin is hidden from the audience both by the angle at which it is being held and by the right hand.

5. As you say "three," drop your right hand to the table and simultaneously let the coin fall from your fingers. The left hand must not open its fingers but simply loosen its grip.

6. From the front, the coin's journey remains hidden behind your right hand.

7. Finish by rubbing your left fingers together and then opening the hand wide to show that the coin has disappeared.

Unlinking Safety Pins

Two safety pins are clearly linked together but, amazingly, unlink three times in a row under challenging conditions. This little routine is an excellent one to learn, as it can be performed impromptu or as part of a larger set, perhaps with some of the other safety pin tricks in this book, such as Pin-credible and Safety Pin-a-tration. Although difficult to follow initially, once you get the knack it is simple.

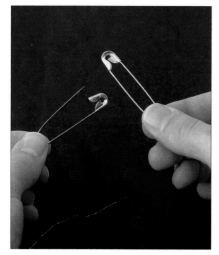

1. Hold one safety pin in your right hand, and open the other. Notice how the open pin is oriented so that the head is to the right and open at the top. (For clarity, this pin has been colored red.)

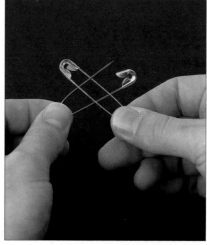

2. Thread this pin through the other. Make sure that the head of the pin in your left hand goes behind the other pin, while the open part goes through the middle. Close the pin.

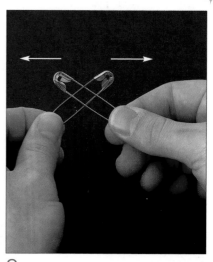

3. Now hold the pins by their ends and pull in opposite directions, as shown by the arrows.

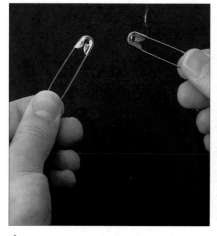

4. The spectator will be astonished that they come apart.

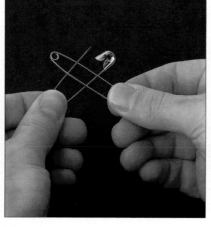

5. You can repeat this trick with a small change. Turn the pin in your right hand the other way up, as shown.

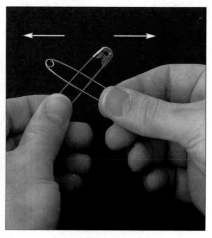

6. Link the pins in the same fashion as before, and pull them apart.

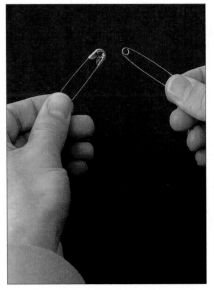

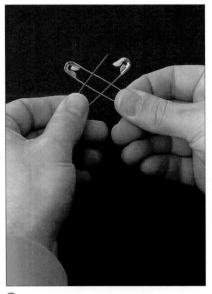

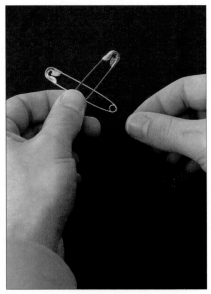

7. The safety pins will miraculously separate again! You can end the trick here, if you like, and hand out the safety pins for inspection, but it is a more impressive sequence if you continue and perform the grand finale.

8. For a finale, link the pins together one last time. However, as you can see, you don't actually link them together at all. The pin in your left hand goes over both sides of the other one, rather than going through the middle.

9. Pinch both pins between the tips of your left thumb and fingers so that the pins stay together.

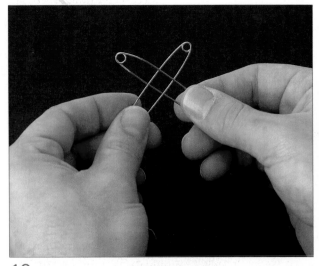

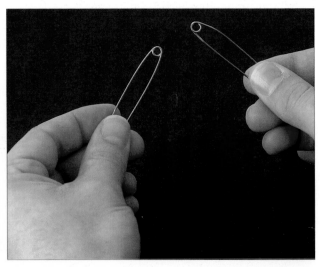

10. Turn the pins upside down, explaining that for the final time you will make the pins penetrate at the bottom instead of the top.

11. Pull them apart. The two pins apparently pass through one another one last time.

Pin-credible

Five safety pins each have a different colored bead attached. You turn your back on a volunteer and hold out your hands behind your back. The volunteer places one of the pins in your hand and hides the rest. You are magically able to divine which color was chosen.

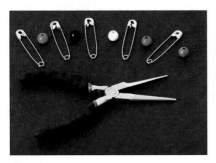

1. Find five beads of the same size but of different colors. You will also need five large safety pins and a pair of pliers.

2. Open all five pins and thread on the five beads. Now you need to prepare each of the pins in a special way that you will be able to recognize.

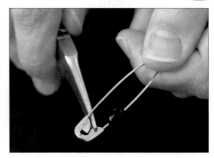

3. Clamp shut the head of the pin with the black bead, using the pliers.

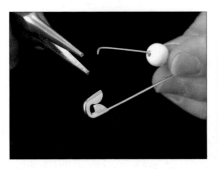

4. Bend the tip of the pin with the white bead threaded on to it.

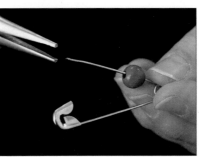

5. Bend the tip of the pin with the green bead in several places, to create a distinct surface.

6. Cut off the tip of the pin with the blue bead. Each pin now looks the same when closed but, when opened, is distinct enough for you to feel which is which.

Secret View

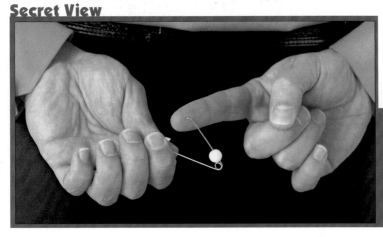

7. With the chosen pin behind your back, secretly open it as you turn to face the spectators again. Depending on what you can feel you now know which color was chosen. Reveal it in a dramatic fashion, and offer to repeat the trick.

Safety Pin-a-tration

A safety pin travels along the edge of a handkerchief before being removed without unfastening the pin. Practice this with an old handkerchief until you understand the principles behind the trick. It will work consistently once you have mastered the moves.

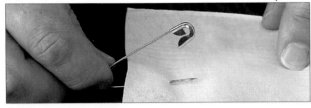

1. Secure a safety pin in the corner of a handkerchief, as shown in the picture above.

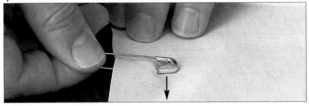

2. Hold the pin with the free top bar flat against the handkerchief, facing toward you. Slide the pin down to the far corner, and the material will slip through the pin's fastener without damage. This is the first phase.

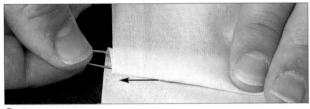

3. Turn the pin over three times, wrapping it in the cloth. Hold the cloth below the pin, and pull it out with your right hand.

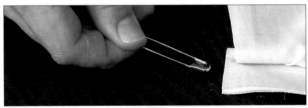

4. The safety pin will come free, still firmly closed, and the handkerchief will remain undamaged in every way.

Domi-no-way

You show the audience that a prediction has been placed in a sealed envelope and then set it to one side. Now you give two people a set of dominoes. Tell them to arrange all the dominoes in any order they desire, making sure that (just as in a regular game) each number matches the number next to it. At the end you ask them to remember the two numbers at the end of the line of dominoes. When they open the envelope, they discover, to their astonishment, that your prediction was correct—a baffling demonstration of your psychic abilities!

1. The swindle is really very easy to carry out. Just remove one domino from a full set, and make a note of the numbers. Then write this out as a prediction and seal it in an envelope.

2. Set the envelope on the table in full view, and ask two people to set out the dominoes as described above.

3. As long as they adhere to the rule that numbers next to each other must match, they will always end up with the two numbers in your prediction at the ends of the line. Show that your prediction matches.

Straw Penetration

Two drinking straws are wrapped around one another and are clearly tangled. Yet with a magical gesture, the straws are pulled apart, leaving both intact. We have used colored straws in the photographs so that the moves are clear and easy to follow.

1. Hold a drinking straw vertically in the fingertips of your left hand and another horizontally in the fingertips of your right hand. The horizontal straw is held in front of the vertical.

2. Wrap the bottom of the vertical straw up and away from you, around the horizontal straw.

3. Continue wrapping it around the horizontal straw, bringing it back over until it is back where it started.

4. Now wrap the right end of the horizontal straw away from you and around the top half of the vertical straw, bringing it back to where it started.

5. Wrap it back over one more time so that the two ends of the horizontal straw meet on the left.

6. Bring the ends of the vertical straw together also, and hold one straw in each hand.

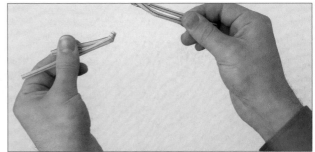

7. Pull your hands apart and incredibly, the straws separate, seemingly penetrating each other. In fact, the order and direction of the twists undo the previous twists, so while they look hooked together, they are really not.

Banana Splitz

An unpeeled banana is magically cut into a number of pieces chosen by a spectator. Cards are used to make the trick more interactive. Allowing the spectator to choose how many times you slice the banana adds another layer of impossibility.

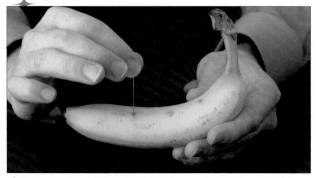

1. Prepare the banana by inserting a thin needle into the skin at three equally spaced intervals along its length and secretly slicing it by moving the needle in an arc. The banana should look normal when you have finished.

2. Place the banana on a plate in front of you and show five cards: an ace, two, three, four and five of any suit. The ace should be the top card.

3. Shuffle the cards, dragging one card off at a time, simply reversing the order. Then repeat, bringing the order of the cards back to the way they were before you shuffled them. Now you need to make a spectator choose either the three or the four. Magicians call this a "force." Deal the cards face down and ask the person to say "stop" at any time as you deal. Time things so that while you are telling him what to do, you deal past the first and second card. He will say "stop" before the last card is dealt and therefore will stop you either at the three or the four.

4. If you are stopped at the four, explain that you will magically chop the banana into four pieces. If you are stopped at the three, explain that you will make three magic karate chops. Mime three karate chops over the banana.

5. Peel the banana and allow the three or four pieces to fall onto the plate.

Kiss Me Quick

A card is chosen by a spectator and shuffled back into the deck, which is then placed back in the box. The spectator blows a kiss at the deck of cards. When the cards are removed, one card is seen reversed in the middle, with a big lipstick mark on its face. It is the chosen card.

1. Prepare the trick by putting a lipstick kiss on the face of a card. You will need a duplicate of this card, which should be placed at the top of the deck.

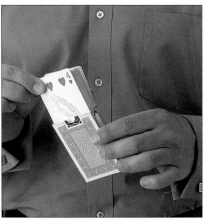

2. Place the deck in the box, with the "kiss" card at one end.

3. To perform the trick, remove the deck of cards from the box, leaving the "kiss" card secretly within.

4. You will now force the duplicate card on to the spectator. (It should be the top facedown card.) Hold the deck on the palm of your hand, and ask the spectator to cut a small number of cards off the deck and turn them faceup, returning them to the deck.

5. Now ask the spectator to cut a bigger batch of cards from the deck, turning those faceup too and replacing the pile once again.

6. Explain that the first facedown card you come to will be theirs. Fan through the deck, and the very first facedown card will be your duplicate. (This technique is known to magicians as the "cut deeper force.")

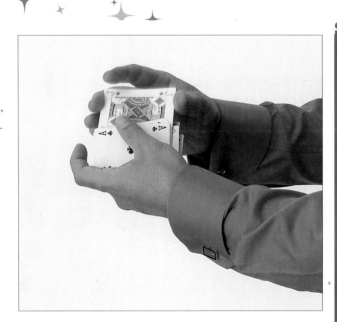

7. Ask your spectator to remember the card and then return it to the deck. Give the deck a shuffle.

Secret View

8. Return the deck to the box. As you insert the cards, be sure that the deck is oriented the opposite way to the "kiss" card, which should be positioned somewhere in the middle of the deck.

9. Ask a female spectator who is wearing red lipstick to blow a kiss at the deck of cards.

10. Remove the deck from the box, and spread out the cards facedown. One card will be reversed, and it will be the chosen card, with a great big kiss on it.

Escaping Jack

You display a card with a hole punched through its center, along with a small envelope with a matching hole. You place the card inside, and secure it with a ribbon running through all the holes. Despite being secured with the ribbon, the card is pulled free and proves to be completely unscathed. If you like, you can substitute the card with a cutout figure of Harry Houdini to add an extra element to the trick.

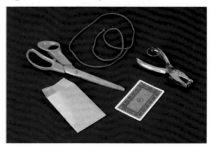

1. You will need an old playing card, a hole punch, a 20 in (50 cm) length of thin ribbon, a pair of scissors and an envelope that is just larger than the card.

2. Prepare the envelope by cutting a tiny sliver off the bottom so that the envelope is bottomless.

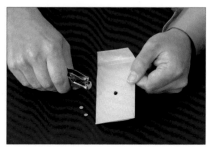

3. Punch a small hole in the center of the envelope.

4. Punch or cut a small hole exactly in the center of the playing card.

5. Show both sides of the card and the envelope to the spectators, and slowly insert the card into the envelope until it is completely inside.

Secret View

6. Give the playing card an extra push so that it starts to emerge from the bottom of the envelope, as shown. The left hand hides this from the front.

7. The card needs to be pulled out far enough to clear the hole in the center of the envelope.

Secret View

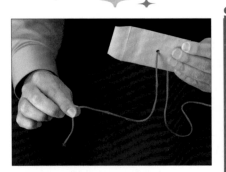

8. From the front, everything looks as it should. Thread the ribbon through the holes in both sides of the envelope.

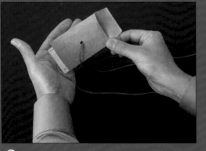

9. As soon as the ribbon is through the hole, push the card completely back into the envelope.

10. This view inside the envelope shows how the ribbon runs over the top of the card.

11. Seal the envelope, and show both sides to the spectators so that they can see that the ribbon goes through it.

12. Grasp the envelope firmly in one hand and both ends of the ribbon in the other.

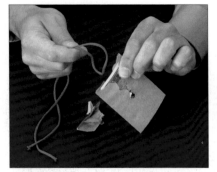

13. With a quick tug, tear the ribbon through the envelope.

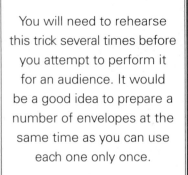

14. Remove the card, and show that it is totally unharmed.

TIP

You will need to rehearse this trick several times before you attempt to perform it for an audience. It would be a good idea to prepare a number of envelopes at the same time as you can use each one only once.

Card on Wall

There is a classic magic trick called Card on Ceiling, in which a chosen, signed card is shuffled into a deck. The deck is thrown in the air, and the signed card flies out of the pack and sticks to the ceiling. The problem is that it can be difficult to get the card down again, and some people object to having a card stuck on their ceiling long after the show is over. So here is a simplified method that looks just as good, which you will be able to use in any venue without ruining the décor. Instead of using the ceiling, you stick the card onto a wall or a glass picture frame. On the other hand, if you have permission or it is your house, you may choose to stick the card to the ceiling. If you throw the card somewhere that can't be reached, the result of your trick will last long after you have left. There will be a story to tell every time someone asks, "Why is there a card stuck to the ceiling?"

1. You will need a deck of cards and a piece of adhesive tape. Make the tape into a loop with the sticky side out. The loop should fit loosely around the middle finger of your right hand.

2. Spread a deck of cards in a fan, for a selection to be made.

Secret View

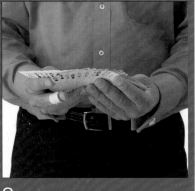

3. Be careful to keep the tape away from the deck.

4. Ask someone to select a card, and remember what it is.

5. Ask her to replace her card on the top of the deck.

Secret View

6. Turn the deck over, and secretly allow the tape to stick to the back of the card. Slip the loop of tape off your finger.

Secret View

7. Prepare to shuffle the deck of cards. Be sure to keep the tape out of the spectators' view.

8. Notice how this overhand shuffle keeps the chosen card in place at the back of the deck. Squeeze the front and back cards every time you take a batch, and the chosen card never moves. From the front, this looks like a genuine shuffle.

9. Prepare to "spring" the cards from your hand by bending them as shown, but don't let the audience see the tape. Aim the cards with the tape pointing directly at the wall.

10. Spring the cards at the wall, and the selection will stick firmly while all the other cards cascade to the floor.

11. The chosen card remains stuck to the wall for a spectacular finish.

TIP

You will probably want to use an old deck of cards for this trick, as the cards will end up all over the floor. Try not to let anyone else remove the card from the surface, or they will see how it is stuck: remove it yourself after the show.

Swapping Checkers

On the table are a column of white checkers and a column of brown checkers. Each column is covered with a paper tube and the two are moved around so that no one knows which color is under which tube. A spectator makes a guess, and the magician shows everyone whether he was correct. Regardless, with a magical wave the two piles change places instantaneously.

1. You will need seven brown checkers, seven white checkers and two sheets of paper. Paint the bottom of one brown checker white and the bottom of one white checker brown.

2. Create two piles of checkers, with the double-sided checker on the bottom of each pile.

3. Use a piece of paper to wrap each column of checkers. The paper should not be too tight.

4. Move the two columns around, sliding the two paper tubes on the surface of the table. Explain that if you don't watch closely, it is difficult to know where each color is. Ask someone to guess where the brown pile is.

5. Whichever pile he points to, tilt both backward and show the colors. Of course, what the spectators actually see is the painted undersides of the prepared checkers.

6. Make a magical gesture as you say that you are going to make the two columns of checkers change places. Lift the paper tube off each pile to show that this has happened.

TIP

For an even better effect, scan one of each color of checker on a computer, print them out at life size in color, and then cut around them and stick them to the bottom of the checkers.

Indestructible String

A length of string is wrapped in a piece of paper. The paper is clearly cut into two pieces and yet the string is somehow completely unharmed. "Cut and restored" is a classic theme in magic; the impossibility of tearing, cutting or sawing something or someone in two and restoring it or them has fascinated audiences worldwide for hundreds of years.

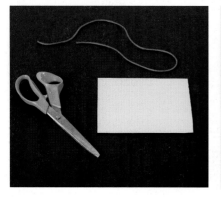

1. You will need a piece of string approximately 20 in (50 cm) long, a pair of scissors and a piece of paper about 4 x 3 in (10 x 7.5 cm).

2. Make a fold about 1 in (2.5 cm) up from the bottom of the paper. Now fold the top piece down so that it just overlaps the bottom edge of the paper. This completes the preparation.

Secret View

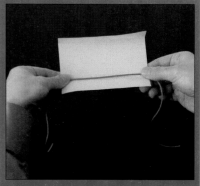

3. To perform the trick, hold the folded paper open, toward you, and lay the string along the lower crease. Notice how the thumbs of each hand pinch the string and paper to hold it all in place.

Secret View

4. Now lift the bottom flap of the paper upward, toward you, with your middle fingers. At the same time, slide your thumbs inward so that the middle of the string becomes a loop.

5. This action is completely unseen from the front.

Secret View

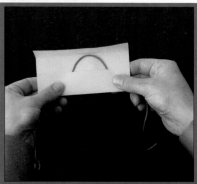

6. Continue to fold up the flap, and grip the string through the paper with your thumbs, as shown here.

Secret View

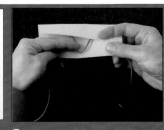

7. Keeping your thumbs still, use your left index finger to pull the loop of string down.

8. Now fold over the top flap of the paper using your right forefinger.

9. Grip the paper and string with your left hand as shown. Pinch the loop of string inside the paper with your thumb to make sure it stays still. Remove your right hand.

10. As you prepare to cut the paper, insert the top blade of the scissors through the loop, and adjust the position of your grip so your fingers straddle the blades and hold on to both sides of the paper. Watch your fingers!

11. From the front, it looks as though you are going to cut through both the paper and the string.

12. With one snip, cut the paper in two. Make sure that the half of the paper in front overlaps the half in the back to hide the intact string and maintain the illusion.

13. Slide the two pieces of paper apart, showing the string intact in the middle.

TIP

If you are left-handed, simply reverse the hand positions so that you can cut using your left hand.

Magnetic Cards

Rubbing your hand on your sleeve to generate static, you manage to stick over a dozen playing cards to your palm-down, outstretched hand. This trick may require a bit of practice in order to perfect it, but once you get used to how the cards are positioned, you will find it easy to succeed every time. There are many different ways of performing this famous and popular trick.

Secret View

1. You will need to be wearing a ring for this trick. Place a tooth-pick under the ring, and keep it hidden as you rub your hand on your sleeve, supposedly to generate static.

2. Hold your hand flat on the table and take the first card, placing it sideways between the toothpick and your fingers.

3. Now add two more cards, as shown, sliding them between the first card and your fingers.

Secret View

4. This view from underneath shows the configuration of the first three cards.

5. Carefully add more and more cards, making a haphazard petal-like pattern, until about twelve cards have been used.

6. Finally, slowly lift your hand into the air, and all the cards will cling to your palm as if magnetized!

Secret View

7. The secret view shows how the cards remain trapped by the toothpick against the palm of your hand.

8. Place your hand back on the table and use your other hand to separate the cards, disengaging the toothpick and leaving the normal cards to be examined by your now amazed spectators.

Picture Perfect

A sheet of paper is torn into nine pieces. Eight pieces are left blank, and a spectator draws a simple picture on the ninth. The magician is blindfolded and by touch alone – apparently from psychic vibes – is able to find the piece of paper with the picture on it. To finish, the magician makes a quick sketch, still blindfolded, and the picture matches that drawn by the spectator.

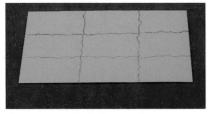

1. Tear a sheet of thin card stock or paper into nine pieces along the lines shown here.

2. Make sure that the tears are not too neat – they should be as rough as possible.

3. Notice that the central piece of card stock or paper is the only one that has four torn sides. This is the key to this trick. Hand out this piece of card stock or paper and ask someone to draw a simple picture on it, keeping it hidden from you.

4. Meanwhile, blindfold yourself using a handkerchief.

Secret View

5. After the spectator has drawn the picture, ask him to mix all the papers together and then to hand them to you behind your back. Take each piece of paper in turn, and feel the edges to determine which piece has four torn sides. This is the one with the picture on it. Bring it to the front and show that you found it.

6. If you are blindfolded with a handkerchief, you will find that you can still see down the side of your nose, even if the blindfold is quite tight. Glance at the picture when you bring it to the front.

7. Make a quick sketch of the same subject while you are still blindfolded.

8. Finish by removing your blindfold and revealing that the pictures match!

Beads of Mystery

Three beads magically escape from two pieces of cord on to which they are tied. This trick is interesting as the method can be adapted for all kinds of tricks, large and small. You will find other tricks in this book that use a similar principle.

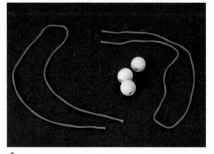

1. You will need three large beads and two pieces of thin cord, each approximately 12 in (30 cm) long.

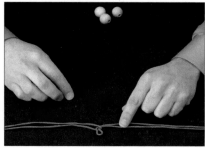

2. Prepare by folding both cords in half and then looping the center of one through the other.

3. Thread a bead onto the right-hand cord, and slip the looped centers inside the bead so that the preparation is hidden.

4. Thread the other two beads onto the cords, one on each side. From all angles it looks as though you have three beads threaded on two lengths of cord. Only you know that the cords are looped.

5. Display the beads on the cord to your audience, and explain that you are tying a knot to make sure they are secure.

6. Hold the cords at either end, and place the beads on the palm of a spectator's outstretched hand.

7. Ask the spectator to close her hand tightly over the beads.

8. Pull on the cords, and the beads will be released into the spectator's hand.

9. After the spectator has opened her hand, you can give everything out for closer examination.

Sweet Tooth

A small paper bowl is shown to contain four candies. It is covered with a second bowl and shaken. The candies are shown to have somehow multiplied so that now there are seven. When the bowls are shaken once again, only four remain.

1. You will need two paper bowls, some double-sided adhesive tape, seven candies and a pair of scissors.

2. To prepare the trick, cut three small pieces of tape and stick three candies to the base of one of the bowls.

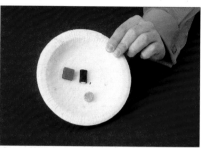

3. The positioning of these candies should look random.

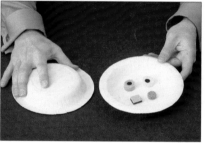

4. In performance, hide the three taped candies by holding that bowl upside down on a surface. Show the other bowl, which contains four loose candies, to the spectators.

5. Cover the bowl containing the loose candies with the inverted bowl.

6. Now turn the bowls over three or five times. As you do so, the candies will rattle inside for all to hear. Because you have turned the bowls an odd number of times the bowl with the fixed candies will now be at the bottom.

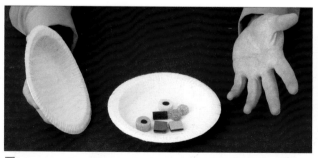

7. Lift the top bowl, showing it to be empty and at the same time asking someone to count how many candies are in the bowl now. Of course there will be three more than before; as the ones that are glued to the base are now included in the count.

8. Finish by either nesting the empty bowl under the other one and removing and eating a candy, or placing the empty bowl over the one containing the candies, and turning the bowl an odd number of times so that the bowl with fixed candies is at the top. When you lift it off, only the four loose candies will be visible.

Ping-Pong Balance

A piece of rope and a ping-pong ball are shown to the spectators. The ball is then magically balanced on the rope and even made to roll backward and forward without falling. Defying gravity is a favorite theme for magicians, and it is used in almost all types of magic. If you can perform this smoothly, it is almost as if the ball is under your complete control.

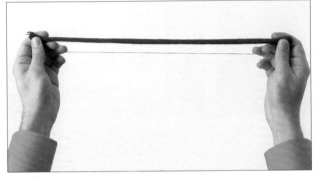

1. Prepare a piece of rope by stitching a length of fine thread of a similar color to it at both ends.

2. Place the ping-pong ball on a stand made from a rolled-up piece of card stock. Stretch the rope out between your hands. The rope and thread should be held as in the previous picture.

3. Lower the rope so that it goes in front of the ball while the thread goes behind it.

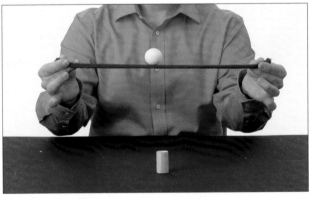

4. Slowly lift the rope, and the ball will look as though it is balanced on it.

5. Tilt the rope gently to one side, and the ball will roll along it without falling off.

6. Slowly lower your hands to return the ball to its stand, and release the ends of the rope.

Zero Gravity

The mouth of a bottle of water is covered with a small piece of paper and inverted. The water remains inside the bottle. The paper is removed, but the water still defies gravity. Finally, toothpicks are fed into the neck of the bottle, proving there is nothing to stop the water from gushing out. This trick takes practice to execute confidently, and it's a good idea to practice over a sink.

1. You will need to make a special gimmick: a disc of clear plastic just a fraction larger than the mouth of the bottle you are using.

2. Punch a hole in the middle of the plastic, and the gimmick is ready.

3. Take a small square of paper, and dip it into a glass of water to wet it.

Secret View

4. You must secretly hold the plastic disc under this piece of paper.

5. Place the wet plastic disc and paper against the mouth of the bottle, and hold it tightly as you turn the bottle upside down.

6. Very carefully let go, and you will find the paper and water remain suspended. Now remove the paper, leaving the disc in place.

Secret View

7. This close-up view shows how the gimmick keeps the water in.

8. Insert a toothpick into the hole in the disc.

9. Watch as the toothpick floats to the surface of the water. This sight is incredible, and it looks like real magic.

10. Finally, turn the bottle upright again.

11. As you do so, secretly remove the gimmick from the mouth of the bottle and hide it in your hand.

Tip

This trick can be done close-up with care, as the disc is invisible at very close quarters. If you want extra reliability, you can purchase a relatively cheap gimmick from a magic shop.

Enchanted Ball

A golf ball is placed on a table, and with the apparent use of telekinetic powers is caused to move all on its own. This trick takes a lot of careful preparation but would work really well if you have friends over for dinner and rig the table before they arrive.

1. You will need a golf ball, a key ring, a needle, some fishing line and a small bead. A large bead and bright thread have been used here for clarity, but you should use thin fishing line and a small bead.

2. Attach a long length of fishing line to the key ring. Set this on a table, and run the line off the far end.

Secret View

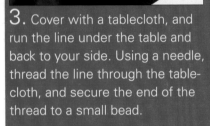

3. Cover with a tablecloth, and run the line under the table and back to your side. Using a needle, thread the line through the tablecloth, and secure the end of the thread to a small bead.

4. Show a golf ball to the spectators, handing it out for examination. Take back the ball and put it on the table, on top of the key ring, which should be invisible under the tablecloth. Engage the bead between your fingers, and strike a pose.

5. Wave your hands over the ball, and slowly move them backward. The ball will start to move away from you. When it reaches the far side, lift it up in the air and toss it out to be examined as you covertly drop the bead behind the table.

What a Mug!

This is a very easy and fun practical joke to play on your friends, which requires just a coin and a mug. Although this trick is a simple "gag," it is the perfect prelude to Mugged Again! and will add an element of humor to the routine.

1. Place a coin on a table, and cover it with a mug. Tell the spectators that it is possible for you to pick up the coin without even touching the mug. When they say they don't believe you, ask them if they want to make a small bet.

2. Say, "It's easy because I never really put the coin under the mug in the first place." When someone lifts the mug to check if it's still there, simply pick up the coin from the table and demand your winnings.

Mugged Again!

This is a perfect follow-up trick to What a Mug! This time you tell the spectators that you will get a from coin under a mug while they hold the mug pinned to the table. You will need to use a little sleight of hand, but it is not too difficult.

Secret View

1. Hold a coin secretly in the fingers of your right hand. Show a similar coin at your fingertips. Place it on the table, and then cover it with a mug.

2. Explain and demonstrate that you are going to get a coin under the mug while she holds her finger on the top of the mug. Keep the other coin hidden in your right hand. This is a view from your angle.

3. From the front the coin remains hidden, and your right hand looks relaxed and normal.

4. Now comes the fun part. Tilt the mug away from you, and reach inside as if you are removing the coin from the table. Actually you leave the coin where it is and push the hidden coin to your fingertips under the mug. It is the hidden coin that you bring into view.

5. From the front it looks just as though you have removed the coin.

6. Now a spectator pins the mug to the table with her finger, and you ask her to close her eyes so she can't see how it is done. When her eyes are closed, tap the coin in your hand against the mug to make it sound as if you are doing something, and then put the coin in your pocket.

7. Tell the spectator to open her eyes and take a look under the mug – the coin will still be there!

TIP

In step 4 do the move without saying anything at all. It should simply look as though you picked the coin up from the table. Try not to call attention to the move.

Magnetic Credit Cards

Have you ever wondered what the magnetic strip on the back of a credit card is for? Did you know that if you rub the strip on your sleeve it will become magnetic? It doesn't really, of course, but your spectators will think so when they see what you do with it!

1. Hold two credit cards, and rub the magnetic strips on your sleeves as you explain to the spectators that you are generating static electricity.

2. Bring the two credit cards together, back to back. The card in your right hand should go behind the one in your left hand.

Secret View

3. Notice how the edge of the credit card is touching the tip of your thumb. Push the cards together, and as you do so allow the card to snap off your thumb and onto the other card. It will look and sound as if they are magnetized.

Secret View

4. Pull the cards away from each other, reversing the movement and pulling the card against your left thumb.

5. Show the audience that the cards are no longer magnetized. If you wish to involve the audience even more, you can borrow the credit cards from a spectator and hand them back afterward.

The Shirt Off Your Back

You ask for a volunteer and sit him down in front of the spectators. Your helper is wearing a shirt and jacket. You ask him to undo his cuffs and the top few buttons. With a sharp tug you pull off his shirt, even though he is still wearing his jacket! This trick requires the help of a stooge: this could be a friend who is dressed ready for action.

Secret View

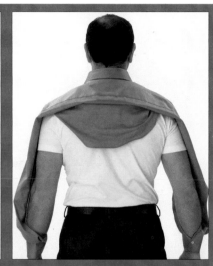

1. An accomplice puts on a shirt in a special way. First, drape it over the shoulders like a cape and button up the top four or five buttons. Then button the sleeves around the wrists.

2. This is how it looks from the back. Try to arrange the shirt neatly so that the fabric is not bunched up in a way that will show through the jacket.

3. Finally put a jacket on over the shirt, and adjust the clothing so that the shirt looks natural.

4. When you perform the trick, invite the supposedly random volunteer to sit down. Stand behind him, and ask him to unbutton the first four buttons of his shirt and his cuffs. The shirt is now loose, and all you need to do is pull with one quick jerk to remove the shirt in an apparently impossible manner. If your friend reacts appropriately, it can be extremely funny.

TIP

To lead into the stunt, you can talk about how you recently saw a TV show about how pickpockets can actually steal the shirt off your back without you noticing!

Unburstable Balloon

We all know what happens when you push a sharp point into a balloon – it goes POP!
Well, with this simple stunt you can push sharp sticks into a balloon without it bursting.

Secret View

1. Blow up a balloon and apply two strips of clear adhesive tape in an "x," as shown. Apply another patch on an area directly opposite.

2. Display a sharp wooden skewer in one hand, and hold the prepared balloon in the other.

Secret View

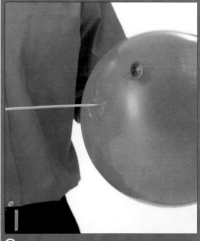

3. Carefully and slowly push the skewer into the balloon, through the center of the tape.

4. Direct the skewer so that it exits the balloon through the second prepared patch.

5. If you prepare enough tape x's on the balloon, you can use several sticks at once.

Obedient Handkerchief

A handkerchief moves around at the magician's command. This can look really funny if your acting skills are good enough. The late Bob Read performed this better than anyone and always had his audiences in stitches.

1. Stretch a handkerchief between your hands. You will find that by holding it through your closed left fist, it will stand up on end quite easily with 4–5 in (10–12.5 cm) protruding.

2. With your free hand, pull the handkerchief higher, and once again, let go. To make it more convincing, look as though you are concentrating on making the handkerchief remain upright.

3. Do this once more until more than half of the handkerchief is upright.

4. With your free hand, motion toward the handkerchief as if you are putting it into a hypnotic trance. Let it fall down, apparently put to sleep as a result of your hypnotic powers.

5. Fold the handkerchief in half, and once again hold it with a section raised through your fist.

6. Pretend to pull a hair from your head, perhaps grimacing as you do so.

7. Wrap this invisible hair around the top of the handkerchief, and pretend to pull the hair. At the same time, push your thumb up, and the handkerchief will bend to the left.

8. Now mime pulling the hair the other way. This time pull down with your thumb, and the handkerchief will bend the other way.

GLOSSARY

adhere To hold fast; stick.

close-up magic Magic that is performed for a small group of people that is standing or sitting nearby, often using small, everyday items.

configuration Arrangement of parts or elements.

covertly Performed in a way that is not openly shown; secretly.

cut and restored An effect in which a magician cuts or tears an object, such as a card, string, or piece of paper, into small pieces and then makes it whole again.

denomination One of a series of values or sizes.

divine To discover or declare beforehand, as if by supernatural means.

force A technique in which a magician controls a spectator's choice (for example, making him or her choose a predetermined card), while giving the illusion that he or she chose freely.

gimmick An object that has been altered to help produce a magical effect.

grand finale The last, and usually most spectacular, portion of a performance.

impromptu Magic that is performed on the spot using everyday items and without any special preparation.

lapping Secretly depositing and hiding an object in one's lap.

mime To imitate.

misdirection Strategy used by a magician to control the focus of the spectator (for example, using a large movement to deflect attention from a smaller, secret movement).

off the cuff Performed without any special advance preparation; impromptu.

penetrate To pass into or through.

pinch vanish A technique used to make an object disappear from view by pinching it so it is hidden by the fingers.

psychic Capable of extraordinary mental processes, such as extrasensory perception.

pull A magic tool that uses elastic to quickly pull an object into or out of view.

rapport Friendly relationship; connection.

sleight of hand Magic that requires quick and skillful movements of the hands.

slide A tube that is used to position an object in an impossible location.

spectator A member of the audience.

stooge Audience member who is planted as part of the act.

telekinetic Able to move objects without contact or other physical means.

Canadian Association of Magicians
Box 41
Elora, ON NOB 1S0
Canada
Web site: http://www.canadianassociationofmagicians.com
This organization promotes and encourages magicians and magic in Canada through magic conventions and other learning and networking opportunities. It is an official member of the FISM (International Federation of Magic Societies).

International Brotherhood of Magicians (IBM)
13 Point West Boulevard
St. Charles, MO 63301-4431
(636) 724-2400
Web site: http://www.magician.org
The International Brotherhood of Magicians (IBM) is a well-respected magic organization with over three hundred local rings, or chapters, worldwide. The organization welcomes amateur and professional magicians, magic collectors, and people with an interest in the art of magic. There are programs and resources designed especially for youth members.

Magicana
15 Madison Avenue
Toronto, Ontario M5R 2S2
Canada
(416) 913-9034
Web site: http://www.magicana.com
Magicana is a charitable arts organization dedicated to advancing magic as a performing art. Its outreach programs for children and seniors employ magic as a teaching vehicle in the community. The organization has a wide range of resources, including a magic collection, classes and seminars, publications, and blogs.

Society of American Magicians (SAM)
Society of Young Magicians (SYM)
P.O. Box 2900
Pahrump, NV 89041
(702) 610-1050

Web sites: http://www.magicsam.com; http://www.magicsym.com
Founded in 1902, the Society of American Magicians (SAM) is a worldwide organization dedicated to the art of magic. The Society of Young Magicians (SYM) is its youth branch, serving people ages 7–17 who are interested in learning and performing magic. SYM has about sixty local "assemblies," or chapters, around the world, including in Canada, South Africa, and Bermuda.

The Young Magicians Club

S12 Stephenson Way
London NW1 2HD
United Kingdom
Web site: http://www.theyoungmagiciansclub.com
FThe Young Magicians Club is the youth branch of The Magic Circle, one of the world's most prestigious magic societies. The club welcomes young people between the ages of ten and eighteen who want to learn the art of magic. Programs draw upon the excellent resources, networks, and knowledge of The Magic Circle.

Web Sites

Due to the changing nature of Internet links, Rosen Publishing has developed an online list of Web sites related to the subject of this book. This site is updated regularly. Please use this link to access the list:

http://www.rosenlinks.com/mag/clos

FOR FURTHER READING

Barnhart, Norm. *Amazing Magic Tricks: Beginner Level* (Edge Books: Magic Tricks). Mankato, MN: Capstone Press, 2009.

Charney, Steve. *Awesome Coin Tricks* (First Facts: Easy Magic Tricks). Mankato, MN: Capstone Press, 2011.

Charney, Steve. *Amazing Tricks with Everyday Stuff* (First Facts: Easy Magic Tricks). Mankato, MN: Capstone Press, 2011.

The Editors of Popular Mechanics. *The Boy Magician: 156 Amazing Tricks & Sleights of Hand* (Boy Mechanic Series). New York, NY: Hearst Books, 2008.

Eldin, Peter. *Magic with Cards* (I Want to Do Magic). Brookfield, CT: Copper Beech Books, 2002.

Eldin, Peter. *How to Do Card Tricks* (Most Excellent Book of—). New ed. North Mankato, MN: Stargazer Books, 2007.

Fullman, Joe. *Coin and Rope Tricks* (Magic Handbook). Laguna Hills, CA: QEB Pub., 2008.

Fullman, Joe. *Sleight of Hand* (Magic Handbook). Laguna Hills, CA: QEB Pub., 2008.

Jennings, Madeleine and Colin Francome. *Magic Step-by-Step* (Skills in Motion). New York, NY: Rosen Central, 2010.

Kaufman, Richard. Knack *Magic Tricks: A Step-by-Step Guide to Illusions, Sleights of Hand, and Amazing Feats*. Guilford, CT: Knack, 2010.

King, Mac. *Mac King's Scout Magic: Over 50 Amazing and Easy-to-Learn Tricks and Mind-Blowing Stunts Using Cards, String, Pencils, and Other Stuff from Your Knapsack*. New York, NY: Black Dog & Leventhal.

Longe, Bob. *Mind-Blowing Magic Tricks*. New York, NY: Sterling, 2007.

Mandelberg, Robert and Ferruccio Sardella. *Mind-Reading Card Tricks*. New York, NY: Sterling Publishing Company, 2004.

Schindler, George. *Presto!: Magic for the Beginner*. Mineola, NY: Dover Publications, 2010.

Zenon, Paul. *Simple Sleight-of-Hand: Card and Coin Tricks for the Beginning Magician* (Amazing Magic). New York, NY: Rosen Central, 2008.

Zenon, Paul. *Cool Card Tricks: Techniques for the Advanced Magician*. New York, NY: Rosen Central, 2008.

INDEX

About the Author

Nicholas Einhorn is a Gold Star member of the Inner Magic Circle. He has won a number of industry awards for his work including: The Magic Circle Centenary Close-Up Magician 2005; F.I.S.M (World Magic Championships) Award Winner 2003; The Magic Circle Close-Up Magician of the Year 2002; and The Magic Circle Close-Up Magician of the Year 1996. Einhorn uses his magic to build crowds for some of the world's largest companies at business trade shows and exhibitions. He has many TV credits to his name and is regularly invited to lecture at magic societies and conventions around the globe. As a magic consultant, Einhorn has designed and created the special effects for several large-scale stage productions, as well as consulted on the film *Bright Young Things*, directed by Stephen Fry. He also develops and markets new magic effects for the magic fraternity. His illusions have been purchased and performed by magicians all over the world, including some of the biggest names in magic, such as Paul Daniels and David Copperfield.